Success in KISS Format

(KEEP IT SHORT and SIMPLE)

Actionable Acronyms
for Life's Journey

PURNA CHANDER

BlueRose ONE.com
Stories Matter
NewDelhi • London

BLUEROSE PUBLISHERS
India | U.K.

BlueRose ONE.com
Stories Matter
NewDelhi • London

For permissions requests or inquiries regarding this publication, please contact:

BLUEROSE PUBLISHERS
www.BlueRoseONE.com
info@bluerosepublishers.com
+91 8882 898 898
+4407342408967

ISBN: 978-93-7139-744-5

Cover design: Yash Singhal
Typesetting: Namrata Saini

First Edition: August 2025

CONTENTS

PREFACE

The aim to write the book is to present the very useful and adoptable actions through thoughts to live a resourceful, peaceful, happy and successful life. Books are the best source to learn and enhance the knowledge.

I have used the technique of ACRONYMS/ MNEMONICS to present the solutions and ways to remember easily. As the title of the book says LEARNING & REMEMBERING is made easy with ACRONYMS/MNEMONICS and the COMMITMENT is expected from the reader and of course DO (practice) part.

Each Chapter is individual in nature and has no connection whatsoever with the each other except the presentation is done in Alphabetical order to facilitate in remembering. The reader is expected to read the chapter and learn the ACRONYMS/MNEMONICS and Commit himself to DO. Unless ACTION is done on anything learnt, there is no use in acquiring Knowledge. Swimming, Cycling or any other skill is learnt only be Practice but never by Theory. My intention is to make it very simple in learning the Thoughts.

GOOD THOUGHTS LEAD TO
GOOD ACTIONS
GOOD ACTIONS LEAD TO

GOOD HABITS
GOOD HABITS LEAD TO
GOOD ATTITUDE
GOOD ATTITUDE LEADS TO
GOOD CHARACTER
GOOD CHARACTER LEADS TO
GOOD DESTINY

The book is a result of years of reading, compilation and create to facilitate the easy learning and utmost care is taken in making it attractive to read by changing the Font sizes, Caps, Bold letters etc.,.

I am grateful to my family, friends and to all with whom I have interacted in my life and to all the various authors of books who have helped me to enhance my knowledge because of whom I am able to write this book.

Thank the readers of the book and wish them an enjoyable reading and expect them to reap maximum benefit from the content and inspire them to follow the **LCD: LEARN, COMMIT, DO** expressed in **KISS: KEEP IT SHORT and SIMPLE** format for **SUCCESSFUL LIVING**

I said Successful Living because as per one definition SUCCESS is "PROGRESSIVE REALISATION OF ONES GOALS WRITTEN ON PAPER". It is a journey not a destination hence SUCCESFUL LIVING

Purna Chander

THOUGHT - 1

ASK: (BEST WAY OF SPENDING TIME)

ASK: ATTITUDE, SKILL, KNOWLEDGE

Time is the common & the only fixed resource available for all. We keep hearing from everyone that don't waste TIME and use it effectively to become successful in life. What is the best way of spending time to become successful? In simple word, since everyone asks the same question, in the word ASK itself there is a way.

ASK: ATTITUDE, SKILL, KNOWLEDGE.

If the time is spent on improving the ATTITUDE, SKILL & KNOWLEDGE, achieving our goals and becoming successful will be a sure shot.

ATTITUDE: Attitude is the Spex of the mind. Like for eyes, the colour of the Spex glass will change the vision, Atttitude is the Spex of the mind. The difference between one another is the attitude which we perceive the world. ATTITUDE brings ALTITUDE. All the self help books, Bhagavadgita, Enlightened Swamis talks etc., all thrive to change the attitude of the person. One sentence or word can change one's attitude. For example if you replace the word PROBLEM with CHALLENGE, the whole perception is changed. If the student is facing difficulty in learning a subject, if he takes it as a challenge than as a problem, his outlook changes completely and he will try to learn it by taking it as challenge.

SKILL: Skill is more connected to ACTION. All the successful sports persons, software & hardware professionals, actors etc., have mastered the skill of doing their job better than others. Tendulkar is an example. He mastered the skill of batting and look what he has achieved. He has mastered playing Leg spin bowling which was his weakness once and he has spared no effort in mastering the technique to play. EVERYTHING IS DIFFICULT BEFORE IT IS EASY. This statement very aptly applies to mastering a skill. Skill is most essential for survival and success in life.

KNOWLEDGE: Everything is knowledge. The child once born is learning everything through various mediums to lead a successful life. Everything including this book also helps us to acquire knowledge needed to live well.

KNOWLEDGE IS MANS GREATEST BEAUTY

KNOWLEDGE IS HIDDEN TREASURE

CHIEF OF EARTHY BLESSINGS, BRINGS

CALM, CONTENTMENT, FAME & PLEASURE.

LCD: There are too many opportunities to get distracted which waste our time and other resources to be unsuccessful in life. Time is greatest resource available to all in equal quantity on a daily basis. If we take one's life, the resource time is same to all. How we use it makes all the difference between one another. This chapter gives a simple word ASK, where if we can check the activity we are engaged is falling in one of the above for SUCCESSFUL LIVING

THOUGHT - 2

AID: (WORDS WITH 100)

AID: ATTITUDE, INTELLECT, DISCIPLINE

If the Alphabets were given the numbers

A -1, B – 2, C- 3…….Z – 26 the words

ATTITUDE: 1+20 +20+9+20+21+4+5=**100**

INTELLECT: 9+14+20+5+12+12+5+3+20=**100**

DISCIPLINE: 4+9+19+3+9+16+12+9+14+5=**100**

AID: ATTITUDE, INTELLECT, DISCIPLINE

As the word AID, Attitude, Intellect & Discipline aid us to become successful in life. Attitude& Intellect are internal and discipline is external skill or a quality which is needed to succeed in life. As mentioned above the surprising common trait of all three words attitude, intellect and discipline, they are total 100. Existential also proves that these three are essential to become successful in life. Attitude& Intellect give you skills to effectively deal with the day-to-day challenges and demands of life. Everyone needs to work on their attitude and intellect by increasing their knowledge on everything to live a peaceful, happy, resourceful and successful life. Discipline is purely external. Motivation is temporary, but discipline is for lifetime. ONE WHO SUBMITS TO

DICIPLINE IS A DISCIPLE. Person has to live life by design not by default. He should plan his day and live accordingly exploiting the time and other resources available to him. Discipline is training your mind not to give a shit if it's hard, or it hurts, or it sucks. If it needs to get done, it gets done. Discipline is an instruction to mind to act, irrespective of the mood or circumstance. Unless something is done religiously, desired results cannot be achieved. Physical, Emotional, Intellectual, Social etc., all areas of life discipline is needed to improve. Unless one is disciplined in his efforts, he cannot expect improvement in his life than before. Discipline is not about forcing yourself to work. It's about creating an environment where work feels natural, a mindset where setbacks are just lessons and a vision so clear that it pulls you forward every single day.

LCD: The word AID itself means that helps. AID: ATTITUDE, INTELLECT, DISCIPLINE are the most vital and need continuous improvement throughout one's life. We should commit to remember and improve them for SUCCESSFUL LIVING.

THOUGHT - 3

ABCD:(NEEDS FOR EXTERNAL IMPRESSION)

ABCD: APPEARANCE, BEHAVIOR, COSTUME DIALOGUE

Appearance, Behavior, Costume and Dialogue are what needs to be followed to make a first impression. They are very important & essential to make a first impression. One should be well dressed well groomed and with a good posture and wear costume appropriately. Well & appropriately dressed individual will definitely have a good impression on others. We need to wear that suits us best. The formal & in formal dress is depended on the occasion. Of course, all official meetings will be formal. Individual's confidence is directly proportional to the attire he is wearing. Well dressed &well groomed individual catches the eye of all. Groomed Hair definitely makes a very good impression. Behaviour is mostly the external body language, gestures and words/language we exhibit. A small gesture can make a lot of difference. Firm shake hand with an erect body posture and a smile on his face reflects confidence. Etiquette and manners are reflected in ones behavior when in many. We need to observe and learn the way other carry themselves when in public.

Observation is one of the best faculty to learn about ABCD. Costume or dress as discussed earlier should suit the occasion. As the occasion demands either formal or informal, colour of the dress, combination of the dress, what you wear on foot is more important as others eye starts observing from the foot onwards. Polished Shoe give a great impression. Excellently dressed with worst maintained shoes gives a very negative impact and impression. Minute details are to be taken care when it comes to Costumes or dress. A missing button on Shirt also can be detrimental to the impression. Dialogue is a final and most important to get positive impression. How and what you say creates a perception on others

LCD: We need to remember ***ABCD*:** APPEARANCE, BEHAVIOR, COSTUME DIALOGUE are vital for a good external influence. The first impression is the best impression, hence we need to commit to follow for SUCCESSFUL LIVING

THOUGHT -4

A^3:(TO MAKE SOMEONE HAPPY)

A^3: ATTENTION. AFFECTION, APPRECIATION

Before the advent of mobiles and other electronic social media platforms, people spent time with each other. Personally, they used to meet each other and spend time by chitchatting. Today most of the people are busy in their own world through mobiles. The need of another human being is not felt due to the World in their hands. Even when together in gatherings, no one is interested to spend time with each other. Each is busy in his own world. But to make someone happy and enjoy our company attention, affection, appreciation is needed.

ATTENTION: Very unfortunate development or rather deprovement is no one pays attention to each other. Even during conversations and social gatherings attention is not given to others. Unless we stop all other activities and listen or be attentive if someone is speaking, it is bad manners and also will greatly disappoint the speaker. The attention to others is a basic trait to make someone special and happy. Even in classrooms the percentage of pupils with attention is dwindling. People are distracted very easily due to the mobiles

AFFECTION: Affection is the minimum we can show towards others for a good relationship. Showing affection to others makes them very happy. Affection towards others, particularly with children& elders makes them very secure and happy. For generation which has not seen Mobiles the indifference of today's Youth disappoints a lot. Even the slightest importance with genuine affection towards them makes extremely happy

APPRECIATION: Appreciation is the minimum expectation of each other to boost the self-esteem. Appreciating others genuinely for their achievements makes them work more towards success. Many do not appreciate or identify the uniqueness of others. Everyone has some uniqueness and we have to recognize that and appreciate and encourage them to become successful.

LCD: A^{3}: ATTENTION, AFFECTION, APPRECIATION are minimum requirements of each other to be happy. We should commit ourselves to genuinely give attention affection and appreciation to others without prejudice. This will help us to have a harmonious relationship and have good impression on us by others to lead a SUCCESSFUL LIFE

THOUGHT -5

CAD:(ESSENTIALS FOR PROGRESS)

CAD: COURAGE, AMBITION, DETERMINATION

These are the traits most important for anyone to face challenges and pays way to successful path. First requisite for anyone to succeed in any field like sports, education, career, etc., Courage is a leading trait. All other traits will follow. We should never bother about the reputation of the others or the opponents in case of games and also for any competition to examination. We should focus on the strategy to be followed. Once the courage is imbibed in the teammates a strong ambition of winning will anchor in their minds. Once the ambition of winning is deeply implanted a fierce determination is created in the teammates mind. For a horse to ride the sides of the eyes are closed to facilitate to see only the front side to avoid any distraction. With courage, a strong ambition is implanted where all the negative traits for success are blocked. When all the self doubts are blocked and total focus on the goal is made, the mind becomes more determined to achieve the goals.

With courage our ambition is strengthened by which a strong determination to win is implanted in the mind. A perfect action plan will be automatically evolved in the mind as the determination of the mind is increased. IF YOU REST YOU RUST.A mind with focus on winning works in the reverse to explore the possibilities of winning at any cost. It becomes a single pointed to achieve success it wanted.

With courage comes ambition. Ambition determines the destination one wants to reach. Without knowing where to go all others traits are useless. We need to know want we want or where to reach. Once that is clear, with courage and determination we can achieve success we wanted.

THOUGHT -6

D³:(PATH TO REACH A GOAL)

D³: DESTINATION, DIRECTION, DETERMINATION

When we wish to go on tour or even to office or anywhere as a matter of fact, we have to decide the destination. In life also until we are students our destination is predetermined as we need to complete each class. But in life for most of the people, it is not clear. Even if destination is decided, the other two Direction & Determination may be lacking. Career, health, weight management, relationship management or in any areas of life, we need to know where exactly we want to reach. Once we decide on the destination then direction of how to reach that goal has to be worked out. A simple example is if someone wants to become an Engineer, he needs to complete his +2 with good percentage and write the entrance very well. Preparation by utilizing all the available resources to achieve the goal is the direction or that destination. To reduce weight & have good health, regular exercise and conscious eating is needed. Many plan up to this level but the most essential determination to be in the same direction to reach the destination is what many lack. A good number of people know what they want and where they want to reach in life but when it comes to the trait of determination, they fail. A simple and most effective way to reach a goal is to write it down and revise it daily. Visualizing the end result will motivate to be in track of the path to reach the goal.

Having a goal book to write the goals in various areas of one's life and the direction to be followed with determination will be very effective. Since 50 to 60 thousand thoughts pass through our mind in a day, it is nearly impossible to stick to one thought without revising and reinforcing that particular thought regularly. Keeping a journal of the goals and revising regularly will reduce the quantity of thoughts and will allow the mind to stick with determination to follow the predefined direction to reach the destination.

LCD: We have lot of inspiring stories in real life which facilitate us to reach our goals.

D^{3}: DESTINATION, DIRECTION, DETERMINATION approach helps us in achieving one's goals written on paper. Some succeed because they are destined to, but most succeed because they are determined to. The best path to SUCCESSFUL LIVING

THOUGHT -7

DREAMSS:(ESSENTIALS FOR HEALTH)

DREAMS: DIET, REST, EXERCISE, AIR, WATER, SUNLIGHT, SELF-CONFIDENCE

DREAMSS, everyone dreams of healthy life. You can have hundred problems in life until you have health problem, then it's the only problem. Health is not just a small part of life, it is everything. The word DREAMS itself has a simple solution of keeping up good Health

DREAMSS: DIET, REST, EXERCISE, AIR, WATER (Used in reverse to have a meaningful word), SUNLIGHT, SELF-CONFIDENCE

DIET:As almost 80% of our physical health and mental health is due to what we eat and think. What we eat place a vital role in maintaining of physical health. Our choice of food and quantity we consume impacts the wellbeing. We cannot prescribe a common diet for all. It depends on the environment, availability and mostly the tradition in the family. Food is more psychological. We should select a diet which suits us both physically and satisfies psychologically. Conscious eating will always help in quantity, quality and digestion.

REST: Rest is very important; particularly sleeping for appropriate number of hours mostly 7 to 8 hours of sound sleep helps the body to recoup. Without proper rest all the other disciplines also will not be very useful. Always aim for good rest in the night and also if needed we should not hesitate to take a nap in the daytime. Sometimes due to excessive strain of eyes or physical the body needs a small nap during the day. The other reasons may be during driving or over eating also body feels like relaxing for few minutes. This will rejuvenate the body immediately after the nap.

EXERCISE: Exercise is very important for all irrespective of age and gender. Having an exercise routine which covers all areas of body internally and externally is very vital for maintaining a good health. (This is dealt in detail in THOUGHT 28).

AIR: Quality Air, which is the most important for well being is also becoming rarity in cities. Pollution due to many reasons is a big issue in cities today. Diseases related with pollution of air have increased tremendously. We need to take precautions to breathe quality and conducive air. Breathing techniques need to be learned to keep our lungs healthy. Already oxygen chambers are there in developed countries. Like bottled water, we can expect Oxygen chambers for a fee in future due to raising pollution in cities and towns.

WATER: Water like air is very important to maintain health. Consumption of a sip of contaminated water is enough to spoil the health of a person. Adequate care is needed to consciously consume purified water.

SUNLIGHT: Sunlight is the most natural and abundantly available health resource in India. In many countries Sunlight is a rarity, but India is fortunate to have abundant sunlight everywhere. It is responsible for many new nutrients like vitamin D. We need to enjoy the sunlight in the morning hours to avoid a good number of health issues.

SELF-CONFIDENCE: Self-confidence though is related to mind is the most essential and first ingredient for success in any field. Without self-confidence nobody can achieve anything because they cannot move forward. The essential quality of the mind to move forward and achieve anything

LCD:DREAMS: DIET, REST, EXERCISE, AIR, WATER, SUNLIGHT, SELF-CONFIDENCE

Having robust health is every ones DREAM. The word itself says the requisites of good health. Just by remembering the word and the expansion of the word, if we can follow all those mentioned above, good healthy body and mind is assured for SUCCESSFUL LIVING

THOUGHT -8

DIN:(ANTIDOTE FOR PROCASTINATION)

DIN: DO IT NOW

'Do It Now' is simple path to success and a good antidote for procrastination which is most difficult to practice. With so many distractions for every one with the advent of technology, networking apps, media, keeping oneself on the task has become challenging. Right from the time we decide to wake up to the time we have decided to sleep, it is literally a fight with ourselves to maintain the schedule. Everyone wishes to utilize the time well but when it comes to overcoming the bad habit of procrastination, seems next to impossible. We need turbo energy to start a task. Why should we practice DIN: DO IT NOW. Our priorities change every day. For students it is studies on the top and others activities will vary. For employees it is attending work and other activities will vary. But every individual has his list of own tasks to complete which will make him more happy and productive. For example, everyone wants to be healthy and wish to do exercise but most of them start with enthusiasm and stop after few days. For students, studies are the top priority but they start some engaging activity like video game or a chat with a friend and end up doing the activity for hours. Prioritizing and sticking to the activity definitely lead to success. The best way to avoid procrastination is just engage on the prescheduled useful activity and mind gets adapted to the said activity. Begin it and the work will be completed. By practicing DIN, our rate of achievement grows leaps and bounds in all the areas of life. At different stages of life, the priorities change. The best way is to have a priority list on daily basis and stick to doing the activities one after the other. This will prevent pressure of performing and also crisis.

LCD: Learning from this chapter is to cultivate the habit of prioritizing the 'to do list' on everyday basis and sticking to do it. Turbo power is needed to start an activity but once started; the probability of completing will be more. If we can avoid the distraction before starting an activity and start to do, we get hooked to it and completing the task becomes easy and this facilitates SUCCESSFUL LIVING

THOUGHT -9

EGO:(GRATITUDE vs EGO)

EGO: EDGING GOD OUT

Edging God out. When someone achieves something he simply forgets the role of superpower or God's role in his success. We are just a speck of dust particle in comparison to the universe and galaxies. There are great many wonders in this universe. Though everyone is unique but can never be greater than the super power, which is the reason for the creation of the vast universe. Everyone irrespective of their achievements during calamity have to pray. PUSH: PRAY UNTILL SOMETHING HAPPENS. Some forget this and feed their EGO on achieving something in this physical world. To state an example for edging God out is: When travelling by bus, if you give someone a seat in between two persons in a two seater, the person tactfully edges out the corner fellow. Likewise, we tend to push off God in our lives in good times. The life itself is a gift from super power or the creator. Every morning when you're able to wake up and stand on your feet is itself is a gift from God. WHAT YOU HAVE IS HIS GIFT TO YOU AND WHAT YOU DO WITH WHAT YOU HAVE IS YOUR GIFT TO HIM. We should always view our achievements or success is, because he wants to do them through us in this world. We are only a temporary image of him to execute our assigned jobs in physical world. Instead of feeling egoistic on achievements, we should cultivate an ATITUDE OF GRATITUDE. With an attitude of gratitude our mind will be peaceful and will facilitate in achieving more. We will become more tolerant, less judgmental and more forgiving. When we observe around, the people with EGO have fallen in life. They have lost everything in life. Some realized and cultivated the attitude of gratitude and reached to better positions than earlier. Initially after achieving success, becoming egoistic feels good and may give you a feeling of pride, but later it is like sitting on a slide, where the person slowly slides down to failure.

LCD: We should learn that ATTITUDE OF GRATITUDE in life helps us to remain grounded in spite of whatever we achieve. Ego will lead to downfall. Let us commit to be always grateful in life even for small things to large things. As said earlier waking in the morning and standing on our feet itself, is a grateful moment. Every day during the wakeful moments and before sleep, auditing the day's activities for the moments to be grateful will be slowly imprinted in subconscious mind and our nature becomes to be with gratitude. Living with an ATTITUDE OF GRATITUDE facilitates us to live peacefully, happily and SUCCESSFULLY

THOUGHT -10

E3:(EXCLUSIVE)

E^3: ENVIRONMENT, EDUCATION, EXPERIENCE

The three external factors: Environment, Education and Experience vary to each individual. Though siblings grow under similar circumstances, the perception or the emotion they store in the subconscious differs. The person's behaviour is through the subconscious impression he stored in the Brain by the E^3 factors.

Environment has wide scope. Culture, Language, Climate, Religion, Region, etc., differ from place to place. The habits people acquire or the living style is picked up from the Environment, Education and Experience they are exposed to. The important and unique character we have to observe is though a set of people like in the same house inmates, classmates of school, etc., subjected to same Environment, Education and Experience, the perception differs from each other. What we perceive or gather from a particular incident is what stays with us. The emotion and perception we pick up stays in our subconscious as memory. We seldom see same reaction from a group of people. No two persons have the same reaction to a situation. These three are most variable external factors which influence an individual in building his personality and character. All the existing differences amongst each other is mainly due to what each perceives from particular incident or situation.

LCD:E^3: ENVIRONMENT, EDUCATION, EXPERIENCE differs from person to person on how we use it in our life. We have to learn to agree to disagree in some situation since each has picked up differently from same situation, by arguing, we can never make others understand our perception. Only by discussion we can try to explain and try to bring others into our way of thinking. By knowing that the E^3 differs for each other and has a tremendous influence on view of life, we will avoid arguments. We will have a harmonious relationship with all since every incident or issue has many dimensions, we should understand that individual has liberty to pick up as per his personality from that particular situation. Learn to understand the uniqueness of the mind of the individual, commit to not to have arguments and do practice this consciously for a SUCCESSFUL LIVING

THOUGHT -11

F³:(TACTFUL LIVING)

F³:FIRM, FAIR, FRIENDLY.

F³:FLIGHT, FIGHT, FREEZE

Our interactions with each other will be on a daily basis. Man is a social animal. He cannot avoid being in the company of other humans. We need to handle difference of opinions, perceptions. Sometimes it will be very challenging to handle human relationships. To have harmony and at the same time conveying our thoughts will be very difficult. The F³: FIRM, FAIR and FRIENDLY approach works very well. We have to practice giving our opinion during conflicting situations in a firm, fair and friendly manner. Our point of view in a situation or during handling subordinates or workmen, fairness, firmness and friendliness will work like magic. Others cannot ignore if our opinion is expressed with these three qualities. Ambiguity leads to altercation. If our thoughts are clear, automatically we will express or lead with firmness fairness, friendliness.

LCD: F³: FIRM, FAIR, FRIENDLY for tactful living. TACT IS MAKING A POINT WITHOUT MAKING AN ENEMY. F³ will help in tactful living and Lead to success,

F^3: FLIGHT, FIGHT, FREEZE.

We encounter variety of situations in formal and informal gatherings. Depending on the situation, we have to use any one of the above to avoid altercation. Sometimes fight only will be the solution, where we need to protect ourselves. Sometimes leaving the situation will be better. Flight, walking away to avoid altercation works well sometimes. We need to grasp the situation and apply the fight, flight, or freeze options. Not saying anything or reacting to certain situations will be very helpful in keeping up with the harmony of the environment. Freeze works well many times if you can avoid expressing our opinion for the issues that do not need our opinion and are not beneficial to us. People always get tempted to express their opinions in spite of others not interested to know.

LCD:F^3: FLIGHT, FIGHT, FREEZE. We have to apply any one of the above, depending on the situation to avoid conflicts. The discretion is entirely on the person and we need to judiciously select one of the options. By learning these options and committing to practice either one of them to avoid disharmony with others for SUCCESSFUL LIVING

THOUGHT -12

FEAR:(DISECTION OF FEAR)

FEAR : FALSE EVIDENCE APPEARING REAL

Most of the time assumptions or over thinking leads to fear. We think that a corner of a rope is a snake. In real life, except for the real situation like an accident or facing an unpredictable animal or exploring an unknown territory, most of our fears are because of our imagination. If we don't study, we will fail an obvious outcome of cause and effect. In situations where ACTION CURES FEAR, it has to be done. To keep health ailments at bay, we have to keep exercising and follow conscious eating. The best antidote for most of the self made fears is ACTION.

C L I P O D : Fear of CRITISM, LOSS OF SOME ONE, ILLNESS, POVERTY, OLD AGE, DEATH

Broadly the major fears are CLIPOD: FEAR OF CRITICISM, FEAR OF LOSS OF SOME ONE, FEAR OF ILLNESS, FEAR OF OLD AGE and FEAR OF DEATH. Other fears like: fear of heights, fear of darkness, etc., are different. They come with birth but the fears we are talking about are self made.

FEAR OF CRITICISM: Our fear of criticism can be avoided while learning to understand that EVERYTHING IS DIFFICULT BEFORE IT IS EASY. Everyone will do mistakes while learning.

Any skill to master needs persistent practice. If we understand this, our perception will change There will always be someone who will not like what we do. So best way is to ignore Criticism and move on.

FEAR OF LOSS OF SOMEONE: Whenever we love someone or dependent on someone, thought of their loss will instill fear in us. The biggest surprise in this life is, anyone can die at any time. Except the creator no knows whose end will come. We are in queue. Neither we can go back or towards sideways. When our time comes, we have to exit this word. This preparation of mind will help us reduce the fear of loss of someone.

FEAR OF ILLNESS: Illness is a major fear. Recent COVID pandemic taught a lesson to many. Most of the deaths were because of fear of infection than the real infection. We need to work on the mind and body to avoid illness. Consistently we have to do exercise and be conscious of the food we take to avoid the fear of illness.

FEAR OF POVERTY: Poverty can be avoided only by work. As long as we are active and working, the fear of property will not arise. Practice of contentment and an attitude of gratitude will reduce the fear of poverty.

FEAR OF OLD AGE: Fear of old-age can be avoided by being active physically and mentally. All have to become old someday. Biological oldness is automatic, but psychological is self made. We are as old as we think. By having an active life, old age can be kept at bay.

FEAR OF DEATH: As stated before death cannot be avoided. We have to cultivate the habit of living joyfully, peacefully every minute of life. Death is inevitable. Our life span is until the next breath. The breath can stop at any time as only the creator knows that. That is the reason we have to live every moment happily, harmoniously, joyfully and peacefully.

LCD: We need to understand that most of our fears are imagination of mind and by over thinking. By becoming courageous and living with self-confidence, a lot can be achieved which facilitates in SUCCESSFUL LIVING

THOUGHT -13

HABIT:(IMPORTANCE)

HABIT: The spelling itself says it is very difficult to change it. If **'H'** is removed **'A''BIT'** remains. If **'B'** is removed **'IT'** remains. Once cultivated, particularly bad habits will be very difficult to change them. EVERYONE IS A BUNDLE OF HABITS. Good or Bad but everyone is more or less a bundle of Habits. Like a system goes into default mode, in the same way many follow a set of habits. Habits are in two categories, GOOD and BAD. Good habits are which lead us to grow in all areas of life. Bad habits are detrimental to us in particular area of life. Habits which facilitate us to improve in **PISES**: PHYSICAL, INTELLECTUAL, SOCIAL, EMOTIONAL and SPRITUAL areas are considered good habits, Regular exercise, reading good books, learning to handle emotions, money management and Satsanga will all lead to happy and Successful living.

GOOD THOUGHTS LEAD TO

GOOD ACTIONS.

GOOD ACTIONS LEAD TO

GOOD HABITS.

GOOD HABITS LEAD TO

GOOD ATTITUDE.

GOOD ATTITUDE LEADS TO

GOOD CHARACTER

GOOD CHARACTER LEADS TO

GOOD DESTINY.

Good thoughts are very important to achieve anything in life. They are the foundation or seeds for good future. Good thoughts lead to good habits through action. Habits make us use the resources effectively to live as per our wish and will. Identifying the habits which suit our life and merge with our lifestyle and then cultivating them with a periodic review of their effectiveness and revising them to reach our goals has to be done. All the successful people are the bundle of habits they cultivated to become what they are. We have to study the Biographies of great men to understand their good habits and try to inculcate in our life, which are suitable to practice. The important factor is what suits. Running in the beach for physical fitness is possible only for the people who are living near shore or the city with the ocean or river. The most important about habit is once it becomes particularly a bad habit, stopping or changing it becomes very difficult.

LCD: We need to learn that man is bundle of habits, hence before cultivating any habit, we need to check how it is going to help us for the betterment in our lives. Sometimes a bad habit like smoking Tobacco or drinking Alcohol start for trivial reasons and suddenly they become very difficult to stop. We have to be very careful before starting something like this even for fun. We have to commit to have useful habits which facilitate us to grow in all areas of our life. Effective utilization of resources in our daily routine helps to in SUCCESSFUL LIVING

THOUGHT -14

H³APJ:(LIFE GOAL)

H³APJ: HEALTH, HAPPINESS, HAMONY, ABUNDANCE, PEACE, JOY

If you look at these six traits, there are more of internal feelings or states of mind. These six are cultivated or can be learned by effort, Ultimate life goals for a successful living.

HEALTH: There is saying that "He is healthy who is not conscious of his body". One day we all have to leave this body but since it is a vehicle we carry as long as we live in it and it needs to be maintained. A planned physical effort and a conscious eating with consistency helps one to be healthy. In spite of efforts, if unavoidable health issues come up, we have to practice not being conscious of body. Apart from being physically fit mind also has to be trained to feel healthy.

HAPPINESS: Happiness is the state of mind. Happiness is not dependent on any external factors. External factors always vary. If you attach happiness with achievement, there will always be something to reach or procure. Though achievements give us satisfaction and happiness but we need to cultivate the happiness state of mind. We should live happily to achieve than live to achieve happiness.

HARMONY: Harmony with everything is needed. This is dealt in THOUGHT 31 in detail.

ABUNDANCE: Abundance is also a state of mind. We all know that one day we have to leave everything we possess and cannot take even a pin with us but still we feel inadequate all the time. Trying to procure too many things will only create nuisance and satisfaction. After working to poses something, the charm of it goes off in few days. An attitude of MORE THAN ENOUGH will help us a lot in feeling abundant. Being happy with what we have and If we can possess more by virtue of hard work with feeling of abundance is okay.

PEACE: Peace is ultimate state we all strive for. We need to execute choice in our thoughts, words and deeds. We need to practice rejection of the thought, word and deed which spoil our peace of mind. We should have absolute control on what we feed in our mind. We should totally abstain externally and internally which spoils our peace of mind. Only peaceful mind will achieve success in life.

JOY: Joy is a blissful state of mind. When you go to being state JOY is experienced. We sometimes, by doing some activity will forget ourself and reach a happy state which is free of thoughts and become joyful.

LCD:H^{3}APJ: HEALTH, HAPPINESS, HAMONY, ABUNDANCE, PEACE, JOY

All the above are independent of what you possess or achieve in life. They are all states of mind. Our ultimate Life Goals. We should practice the methods to achieve the above states of mind for SUCCESSFUL LIVING

THOUGHT -15

IDEAL:(PROBLEM SOLVING TECHNIQUE)

IDEAL: IDENTIFY, DEFINE, EXPLORE, ACT, LOOK BACK

Everyone in life wishes to live without problems but it is very difficult to imagine anyone's life without facing any problems With major areas of life, being PISES: Physical, Intellectual, Social, Emotional and Spiritual, we have some issue or the other in any of these areas which needs to be resolved. **IDEAL**: IDENTIFY, DEFINE, EXPLORE, ACT, LOOK BACK is a perfect step by step technique to solve the problems faced in any area of life. First, we should identify the reason for facing the problem. Example: Physical Fitness. Today Obesity or health issues are very common. We all know the Diet, Exercise and meditation will resolve the issue. We need to define the problem, whether it is because of Overeating or sedentary life style. After identifying the problem we need to define it correctly. Once it is defined, we have to explore the possible solutions to solve. There will be many solutions, but all may not be working. FOR EVERY AILMENT UNDER THE SUN, THERE IS A SOLUTION OR THERE IS NONE. IF THERE IS ONE TRY TO FIND, IF THERE IS NONE

FORGET IT. After exploring the various solutions, we have to act. Any problem is solved only when we take action. ACTION IS THE ONLY CURE FOR MANY PROBLEMS. The perfect action is not found in the first attempt. We need to look back and assess the problem. In the sequence of IDEAL problem solving technique all the steps are needed to solve the problem. Obesity, not being able to have a satisfactory career, failing to maintain harmonious relationships, etc., are some of the problems faced by too many people.

LCD: Learn the sequence of techniques IDEAL: IDENTIFY, DEFINE, EXPLORE, ACT, LOOK BACK to solve the problem and commit to follow the same procedure for every type of problem in any area. Need to explore the various solutions until we are free of the problems. The IDEAL step by step technique to solve the problems will help in SUCCESSFUL LIVING.

THOUGHT -16

I CAN:(BEST ATTITUDE)

ICAN is the best attitude to achieve anything. When we think 'I CAN' we will work with the end mind. We will work backwards to achieve the goals. There are three sorts of people I WILL, I WON'T, I CAN'T. I will achieve anything. I won't oppose everything and I can't fail in everything. I will, I can attitudes give a tremendous strength of mind and will show the direction to achieve the pre-written goals. With I CAN attitude problems will be looked as CHALLENGES and failures will be as FEEDBACKS. The whole paradigm changes when we see any obstruction as a challenge than as a problem. A Problem may not have a readymade solution but a challenge will create solutions. Challenge itself is such a positive word that a person will never let It go unachieved. In that frame of mind failures are looked as feedbacks which allows the mind to look into various possibilities of achieving one's goals. Life itself is very challenging. In all phases and all areas of life we encounter so many obstacles that many lose the will to achieve and most of them drop off at the obstacles, but if the attitude of I CAN is cultivated, though late but the goals will be achieved. For most of the people all life goals are beaten tracks. Will power is sufficient to reach the destination. But for the Stalwarts who created Airplane, Trains, Motor cars, Mobiles etc., it was totally unknown territory but they invented them with sheer will power and absolute faith on themselves. In spite of the impossibilities of things, all the inventions which we are enjoying was achieved only with the attitude of I CAN.. The moment the mind is cultivated to see only the possibilities of accomplishing something then only it becomes a reality. Every success in sports, music, etc., was possible only with the belief of the doer. That is the reason we see only handful of people at the top with achievements which are difficult to believe. Competing the 100 Meter race in less than 10 seconds took some decades to achieve but once it is done by one man, now hundreds have done it. The mind also believes and follows an example very easily.

LCD: We have to understand that I CAN attitude will facilitate reaching goals and ambitions by showing the direction. Commit to subconsciously imprint in the mind I CAN ATTITUDE which leads to SUCCESSFUL LIVING.

THOUGHT -17

KAIZEN:(FORMULA FOR SUCCESS)

KAIZEN: KEEP ALWAYS IMPROVING WITH ZEAL and ENTHUSIASM WITH NO LET UP

Life of purpose and purpose of life. Constancy of purpose. The main obligation and possibility of being human is to improve than before. Our main aim in life is to improve or better ourselves in all areas of life than before.

I HAVE NO YESTERDAY'S,

TIME TOOK THEM AWAY.

TOMORROW MAY NOT BE

BUT I HAVE TODAY.

What you can do today or rather now in life matters. No one can bring back yesterday or can go to tomorrow. What we do this moment is what matters. And the best way is 'TO LEARN FORM THE PAST, ACT IN THE NOW and PLAN FOR THE FUTURE. If you keep on improving ourselves in all the areas of life like physical, intellectual, social, emotional, and spiritual life, the best version of ours will be evolved. LIFE IS A JOURNEY: NO BEGINNING, NO END. JUST A FLOW, PERENNIAL USEFUL FLOW. If we are conscious of our thoughts, actions will follow. To achieve anything in life applying this formula KEEP ALWAYS IMPROVING WITH ZEAL and ENTHUSIASM WITH NO LET UP makes it possible. Any great achievement is of small steps.

LITTLE DROPS OF WATER

LITTLE GRAINS OF SAND,

MAKE THE MIGHTY OCEAN AND

THE MIGHTY EARTH

LITTLE MINUTES THOUGH THEY BE

MAKE THE MIGHTY AGES OF ETERNITY.

For anything to achieve it is the little efforts which produce great results over a period of time. LITTLE PROGRESS ADDS UP TO GREAT RESULTS. The effort should have enthusiasm, hope, faith and determination. Consistency is a mantra in any achievement. 99% lack this quality of consistency. Many start on the path to achieve their goals but a small obstacle or lack of Will power, they drop off in a few days. They stop their efforts. Without consistency, we fall back from more than what we have achieved till date.

LCD: Learn that minor improvements in our efforts in all areas lead to success in life. Commitment to stick to the routine is important. We need to visualize ourselves reaching our goals and imprint in our subconscious mind that **KAIZEN:** KEEP ALWAYS

IMPROVING WITH ZEAL and ENTHUSIASM WITH NO LET UP is the mantra for SUCCESSFUL LIVING.

THOUGHT -18

KISS:(TECHNIQUES TO ACHIEVE)

KISS: KEEP IT SHORT and SIMPLE

Today the attention span of all has come down to minutes. Instagram reels, WhatsApp videos etc., are concise. Many are uploading giving information in the concise videos. I have adapted this technique in this book to explain and facilitate remembering to LCD: LEARN, COMMIT, DO in life to live successful and to achieve their goals. Abbreviations or short forms of the information will facilitate remembering and recollection to apply in day-to-day life. All 40 THOUGHTS have been designed in the same way. Every area of life like health, time, interpersonal relationships, influences of life, techniques to achieve goals, ultimate aim of life, etc., have been covered and stated in KISS FORMAT. For example: If one wants to have good health, THOUGHT 6 DREAMSS explains what needs to be done. Categories of human relationships are explained THOUGHT 19, Broadly the areas to be improved on daily basis is explained in THOUGHT 24.Resources and how to effectively and efficiently use them is explained in THOUGHTS 25,36 and 39.Characteristics of goals in THOUGHT 30,Harmony with what is essential in THOUGHT 32, the filters for conversations and how to talk effectively is THOUGHT 35,Time management in THOUGHT 36, What needs to be followed in raising the children in THOUGHT 38,Resources management in THOUGHT 39 and the last chapter 40 gives a gist of what should be done by all.

Learning and increasing knowledge is one aspect but remembering and recollection and applying the knowledge is other aspect. Unless applied, the knowledge is useless. KISS format helps us to remember easily and applying at the right time has to be consciously practiced.

LCD: Learn the knowledge given in the form of KISS format in this book. Commit to practice them till they are implanted in the subconscious mind. Whenever a problem or challenge is faced in that particular area, we have to apply this knowledge. THOUGHT 14 **H^3APJ**: HEALTH, HAPPINESS, HAMONY, ABUNDANCE, PEACE, JOY are the ultimate life goals to be achieved for SUCCESSFUL LIVING

THOUGHT -19

LRS:(DIMENSIONS OF RELATIONSHIPS)

LRS: LIFE TIME, REASON, SEASON

Human relationship can be classified in only three categories. LRS: LIFE TIME, REASON, SEASON. Though it is surprising but any interpersonal relationship falls under one of the category.

LIFETIME: Lifetime relationships are blood relationships. Parents, Children, Grandparents, Uncles, Aunts, Cousins or any relationship which has become due to virtue of being born into the said family. Wherever you are unless you wish to not to have that particular relationship it stays for lifetime. Relationship with parents, children or siblings is because of divine connection. We see people not being happy if they're not harmonious with immediate lifetime relationship. Something bothers you very strongly in the subconscious mind if there is disharmony in the lifetime relationships.

REASON: Second category is Reason. While travelling in public transport or during planes or train journeys, we make a temporary relationship with co-travelers. Majority of those relationship relationships are gone once our journey is done. Due to communication facilities some may continue for a period. But it is very rare to see them continue. Those relationships happen only due to a reason. Travel or otherwise, the least importance can be given to these type of Relationships to continue.

SEASON: Seasonal relationships are the third category. Classmates of school or college, co-tenants, neighbors', colleagues come under this category. They are there are for a time period, it can be days, months or years but most of them vanish after period of time. As said earlier, unless we wish to continue, there will not be any substantial reason to continue the season relationship after the particular time.

LCD: We need to understand what type of relationships we have to maintain it harmoniously. Lifetime relationships need to be maintained harmoniously as they affect our day-to-day life. Not having harmony with parents, siblings, children and close relatives will definitely have stress in life. We definitely need to have more tolerance to maintain lifetime relationships. Relationships which are made for a reason can be ignored because either ones will not bother to continue the relationship as it is temporary. Seasonal relationships need a slightly mature approach and need to be maintained with the principle of sustain and abstain. We have to assess the type of relationship and take adequate measures to have harmony for SUCCESSFUL LIVING

THOUGHT - 20

MATE:(PURELY PERSONAL)

MATE: MEMORIES, ATTITUDES, TALENTS, EXPERIENCES

MATE itself means someone who stays or a friend of us. AMATE is exclusive each one.

MEMORIES: Memories are totally personal in nature. No one's memory matches with others. The same incident witnessed by more than two persons has different memory to each other. Memories are individual. What we perceive remains and it will always be different with others. Perceptions are never the same. Everyone acts through his memory which he perceived at the time of incident. During all phases of life, only a few are very strongly imprinted in the mind.

ATTITUDE: Attitude is what we see the world through one's MEMORIES, THOUGHTS, EXPERIENCES. Attitude is also totally independent in nature. Though ATTITUDE BRINGS ALTITUDE, what sort of THOUGHT SPEX one has, no one can say. Attitude is the result of one's thoughts very strongly implanted in the subconscious mind. Our behaviour or reaction to a situation is because of attitude. That is why ATTITUDE BRINGS ALTITUDE. Attitude can be cultivated by feeding good thoughts to the mind. Attitude is responsible for many traits in all.

TALENT: Talent is unique to each individual. No two persons talents are same. Few Talents are God gifts for example: Singing But talent, if recognized early, can be nurtured to perfection. If natural talent is found early, can be cultivated to achieve and become best in that particular field. Sports, Arts, Games, etc., are all talent based. Only few will be lucky to recognize the inborn talent and nurture to attain greatness through exhibiting.

EXPERIENCES: Experiences are again exclusive. No two persons perceive exactly the same way when witnessing an incident. The experiences recorded in the mind are definitely different with one another. The attitude is also the result of experience one has in life.

LCD: Learn to understand that MATE: MEMORIES, ATTITUDES, TALENTS, EXPERIENCES are unique in nature. Hence no two persons have the same opinion on anything. Many times it is better to AGREE TO DISAGREE due to the unique perceptions. Once we understand this, we will reduce to fight to make others accept our opinions. If you are conscious of the difference and uniqueness of individual MATE: MEMORIES, ATTITUDES, TALENTS, EXPERIENCES our attitude towards life changes and leads to SUCCESSFUL LIVING

THOUGHT -21

MAT:(EXTERNAL INFLUENCES)

MAT: MAJORITY, AUTHORITY, TRADITION

Place of birth decides many external and internal factors of a person. Geographical place has a major factor for the habits and attitude. To sum up the external influences majority, authority and tradition affect the life of all. In the vast world, every area has uniqueness in many things. There are so many cultures, rituals and traditions followed by time immemorial due to the influence of majority. Place to place, country to country, city to city, these external influences differ. What followed by majority generally becomes the norm of the particular sect or area. It will be very difficult for anyone to oppose the decisions of majority in many instances. Traditions are also followed depending on the birth in that particular section or sect of the society. No one can go against the traditions as they are blindly followed by generations. Traditions, vary depending on the parameters, like caste, creed, place, country, rural, urban, male, female etc.,. Tradition is so strong that no one questions. The elders pass on the traditions to younger generations. There may be reason for the particular traditions or not but no one dares to question them. Authority can be by virtue of inheritance or elected or by majority but even authority cannot be questioned. Authority is generally present by caste, creed, place, country, rural, urban, male, female etc.,. Authority is also very big external influence in our life like each human being is unique. Majority, Authority and Tradition are unique for the variables of caste, creed, place, country, rural, urban, male, female etc.,.

LCD: We should learn that the MAT: MAJORITY, AUTHORITY, TRADITION are external influences, which need to be considered in one's life and intellectually adapted to facilitate realization of one's goals in life. No one can oppose and live peacefully with a shift in majority, certain practices are abolished or changed but it is not always possible. To go against **MAT,** it needs lot of factors like more number of people should be willing to oppose. Unless it affects the society in a negative way, we should go with the flow and follow the **MAT:** MAJORITY, AUTHORITY, TRADITION for SUCCESSFUL LIVING

THOUGHT -22

MBA:(MUST FOR PROGRESS)

MBA: MARKET YOUSELF, BE IN LOVE WITH YOU, ALWAYS LEARN

Normally MBA means MASTER OF BUSINESS ADMINISTRATION. Here we have a better formula of progress.

MARKET YOUSELF: As said many times earlier, everyone is unique. Unless we market our uniqueness, no one will be aware of us. Most of the successes are because of RIGHT TIME AT THE RIGHT PLACE. Everyone has to market their special capabilities that will facilitate for others to know and when the time comes or need arises, an opportunity will be given. Unless a person marketshis capabilities, no one will know. Exposure to others is very important. Today the world has become very small due to technology. Marketing the talent is not very difficult. Opportunities come to the person with more exposure.

BE IN LOVE WITH YOU: Unless we like and love ourselves, our personality will be either with low self-esteem or over confident. Every person has three variations. WHAT OTHERS THINK OF HIM, WHAT EXACTLY HE IS and WHAT HE THINKS HE IS. What he is and what he thinks he is, are not matching then that will lead to either low self esteem or over confident., We need to have a balanced personality with matching of what we are and what we think we are. Acceptance of ourselves with total conviction is needed to progress in life. Unless we love ourselves we cannot love others. Nothing great can be achieved without accepting and loving ourselves with all our strengths and weaknesses. We have to accept ourselves. We have to work on our traits and do SWOT (STRENGHTH, WEAKNESS, OPPORTUNITIES and THREATS) analysis to accept ourselves completely.

ALWAYS LEARN: We should try to better ourselves than before. This needs learning continuously. Learning and improving in all the areas of life should be our passion. We need to work on all areas to get to become better version of ourselves than before. Learning is the most essential quality to succeed in life. EDUCATION IS DEFINED AS THE MANIFESTATION OF PERFECTION IN MAN. Perfection is process of Evolution. No one is perfect but everyone can strive to become perfect in their life by learning continuously.

LCD: Learn that whether you do MBA or not, but we have to follow the life **MBA:** MARKET YOUSELF, BE IN LOVE WITH YOU, ALWAYS LEARN. These three qualities are for lifetime. They need to be practiced for life time. The effort of this book is always to take care of the 'Always learn'. We should have our eyes and ears open to utilize the opportunity to MBA: MARKET YOUSELF, BE IN LOVE WITH YOU, ALWAYS LEARN for successful living.

THOUGHT -23

MYOB:(CONFLICT AVOIDING)

MYOB: MIND YOUR OWN BUSINESS

This principle if learnt will facilitate avoiding conflicts. Many times people get tempted by "If asked by me" and they will interfere in unnecessary matters and get it to conflict and altercation. If the society is facing an issue and the majority are opposing then we have to express our solidarity. But in Mundane issues, many get tempted to throw their weight and get caught in conflicts. Many times our opinion is not needed among the conversations either at home, office or other gatherings but most of the time people get tempted to give their opinion which may lead to altercation. NO ONE HAS EVER WON BY ARGUING. The best way to avoid is to MIND YOUR OWN BUSINESS. Even when asked for the opinion, if we really are able to defend our opinion with perfect knowledge on the subject, we should express it. The best way is to skip it as it will give us peace of mind. Arguments always lead to conflict. No one can really win an argument. In case of an altercation or conflict, the best way is to AGREE TO DISAGREE. There will be situations where not saying something is also not correct. In those situations we should TACTFULLY express our opinion. TACT IS MAKING A POINT WITHOUT

MAKING AN ENEMY. Peace of mind in interpersonal relationships is possible only when we have harmonious relationships. Unwanted expression of our opinion will most of the time lead to conflict with others. Some topics like politics and religion where emotions are predominant in opinions, the relationship can be spoiled beyond repair. The temptation to express ourselves will be very dominant but nothing like restraining ourselves to avoid conflict is the best option. Practice to restraint ourselves from unwanted conversations is needed.

LCD: We have to very strongly inculcate the thought of **MYOB**: MIND YOUR OWN BUSINESS in the subconscious mind to avoid interfering in the discussion or conversations of others. Unless asked we should be able to skip with a smile. When this thought is practiced even for a day, the benefit will be visible. We have to commit to **MYOB**: MIND YOUR OWN BUSINESS to avoid conflicts for SUCCESSFUL LIVING.

THOUGHT -24

PISES:(AREAS FOR IMPROVEMENT)

PISES: PHYSICAL, INTELLECTUAL, SOCIAL, EMOTIONAL, SPIRITUAL

Everyone has these dimensions in life. The main obligation or duty of anyone is to improve himself than before in all the dimensions of one's life.

PHYSICAL: Physical dimension is tangible in the form of body for every human being. It is called TEMPLE. Birth to death one has to live in the physical body and identity is only through physical appearance first. Physical health and appearance have to be maintained and need to be improved on a daily basis. Without physical fitness all other areas are useless. Regular exercise and conscious eating are very important for physical area improvement.

INTELLECTUAL: Intellect is again an important area. Intellect is not tangible. It can be felt only by our actions or reaction to a situation. Intellect is to be cultivated. It is responsible for one's success in life, profession and career. Intellect has to be improved regularly to facilitate facing the challenges of life. With intellect Life's challenges can be faced and can be won over.

SOCIAL: Man is a Social animal. He cannot live alone. He needs society to live. Human Social needs are many. Recognition, Appreciation, Attention, etc., are some of the self-esteem needs of the human being. Harmonious relationships are basic social needs of all. Interpersonal relationships are very challenging. Everyone has to learn the social skills to have harmonious relationships with each other. Skills of social engineering need to be improved on a daily basis. With raised psyche's of humans, adept social skills need daily learning.

EMOTIONAL: Emotional quotient (EQ) differs from person to person. Man is a bundle of emotions. Learning to control or handle emotions is a skill to be mastered. We have to audit our emotions on regular basis to learn to have absolute control on our emotions. Extreme emotions will create blunders. The behaviour is totally in the control of one's emotions. A person with no emotional control will be unpredictable and will be a nuisance to deal with.

SPIRITUAL: Spiritual quotient (SQ) in other important area. To believe God or not itself is a big issue. Being spiritual will create peace and harmony in life. Spiritual area needs daily practice. There will be always something unanswered. The differences in life are always a mystery for any. Continuous study, revision and meditation is needed to understand the spiritual area of life.

LCD:PISES: PHYSICAL, INTELLECTUAL, SOCIAL, EMOTIONAL, SPIRITUAL. Broadly all humans life has the above variations. A CANI:

CONTINOUS AND NEVER ENDING IMPROVEMENT in all areas is needed for all to evolve into perfection which is the ultimate goal of any one. Thoughts followed by actions in all areas are needed for SUCCESSFUL LIVING

THOUGHT -25

PEEP:(SPACE MANAGEMENT)

PEEP: PLACE FOR EVERYTHING AND EVERTHING IN ITS PLACE

In Universe we see everything is in its place Defined place is found for everything. Even in our body, every part is so designed that any change will create a big issue in the body. One of the major resource of mankind is space. All the resources are discussed in THOUGHT 39.For our day-to-day life, we have a space to stay, a space to work, a space for Entertainment, a space to keep our things at home and at office. How effectively we use the space is directly proportional to the success. Every day we use so many items for daily use clothes, belt, shoes, pens, Keys, etc.,. The list would be too long. If a person does not have the habit of managing his things in the available space, he will be wasting his time searching for it. We have to cultivate the habit of allotting a place for all our belongings and keep them in those places after we use. Organizing and planning may take some time but the habit of PLACE FOR EVERYTHING AND EVERYTHING IN ITS PLACE helps us to live effectively. At all stages of life, the items of usage may change like for students, it will be school uniforms, shoes, etc., for employees, it will be files, bag, etc., for old people, it will be medicines, clothes, and other items. There will be many but I am just mentioning as an example. As per the requirement at that stage of life, we should allot the place in the space available for the things and need to cultivate the habit of placing them after use at the allotted spaces. This will make life very smooth and frictionless. This habit seems very trivial but it helps in organizing the important resource of space very well. Effective usage of the resource where the time on miscellaneous is saved and used for progress will definitely lead to success.

LCD: **PEEP**: PLACE FOR EVERYTHING AND EVERTHING IN ITS PLACE helps in organizing things very efficiently and effectively. The habit to cultivate may seem trivial and also difficult initially but once cultivated lead to SUCCESSFUL LIVING.

THOUGHT -26

P²:(TWO EXTREMES)

P² : PAIN & PLEASURE

For any activity the result is either pain or pressure. The main outcome is either of two. If we divide habits into good and bad, most of the bad habits give instant pleasure but end up with pain. Good habits give instant pain but end up with pleasure. In any area of life at any stage, the biggest motivating factor for an activity is pleasure. All will try to do activities which give them pleasure but the surprise is most of the bad habits give instant gratification and the end up with tremendous pain. That is why we need to choose the habits or activity which may give you pain doing it but end up giving us a drastic positive change to end as pleasure.

We are conscious of this since we were young but until schooling starts the life goes by the motivation of instant pleasure. Once the schooling starts the immediate result of pain to study stops us from doing it. Most of the students waste their time with mobile, TVs, watching movies, etc.,. But the result will be painful because they are motivated by pleasure giving activities. The wise thing to do is to stick to smart and hard work, which may be painful to study but give result of pleasure. Every students desires good grades or marks in studies but unless efforts are not put the result will also be disappointing. Though the outcome of all activities is either pain or pleasure, the wisdom of choosing immediate gratification or long-term is needed. Even physical exercise which keeps fit, healthy and agile is painful while doing it but at the end, the pleasure it gives is un measurable. That is the reason why many do not like good advice is because they are addicted to the immediate pleasure an activity gives. Today due to social media, most of the students, adults and others are hooked to enjoy the pleasure it gives and the result is disastrous. A good part of the prime time and life are wasted in the useless activity. The young adults are unable to select the positive good habits which are painful while doing but give us pleasure in the long run.

LCD: All activities are only two outcomes

P² : PAIN & PLEASURE. Mostly immediate pleasure activities end up painful and immediate painful activities end up with pleasure. We should use our discretion to select those thoughts which lead to good actions which lead to good habits which end in the result of achieving our goals for SUCCESSFUL LIVING.

THOUGHT -27

P^3:(BEST QUALITIES)

P^3: PURITY, PATIENCE , PERSEVERANCE are the best qualities to have peaceful, harmonious and successful life.

PURITY: Purity where the THOUGHT, WORD, DEED are same of a person we can call he is a pure soul. Most of the time, we see that people have something in the mind and they do opposite of that as a word or deed. Intention is the function of communication but deliberately most of the people have cultivated a habit of thinking opposite of their words and deeds. They appreciate with words, hug a person but in the minds they have animosity. This is never called Purity. This will one day be exposed as the intention will be discovered. Purity is a noble quality and needs a lot of courage to practice. Purity is achieved by aligning THOUGHT, WORD & DEED.

PATIENCE: Patience is a one quality which separates achievers and non-achievers, matured and immature, tolerant and intolerant. Patience is a quality to be cultivated to become successful in life. For everything in life a proper time for evolution is needed. Even a baby takes nine months to take birth since its formation. Every activity to become successful, patience is needed. Learning a skill, acquiring, knowledge, etc., need a minimum time to learn. Patience is a quality where it reduces the enemies. Patience is a solution for many alterations at all places. Harmonious relationships are mostly due to patience of both or even one in a family. Patience is a quality or trait which can be cultivated. Patience also comes by age as experience teaches us that it can solve many issues. For all most all of our activities Patience is prerequisite for success.

PERSEVERANCE: Perseverance is another best quality for everyone to achieve anything in any field. Apart from purity, patience, perseverance is also very important. EVERYTHING IS DIFFICULT BEFORE IT IS EASY. Any skill can be mastered by perseverance. Consistent efforts to learn is the only key for success. PERSEVERANCE IS A GREAT ELEMENT OF SUCCESS. IF YOU KNOCK LONG ENOUGH AND LOUD ENOUGH, YOU ARE SURE TO WAKE UP SOMEBODY.

LCD: The best qualities anyone can have to live a successful life are P^3:PURITY, PATIENCE and PERSEVERANCE. We should commit ourselves to be pure, patient and perceive on whatever goals we have written to achieve. All these qualities can be cultivated with efforts. All great achievers had these qualities. SUCCESSFUL LIVING is possible only by practicing and improving PURITY, PATIENCE and PERSEVERANCE..

THOUGHT -28

P^4:(SINGLE FORMULA FOR ACHIEVEMENT)

P^4: PERSISTENT PRACTICE PROMISES PROGRESS

To achieve expertise in any skill the basic need is to practice it at every opportunity consistently. All achievers in sports, music, etc., had years of consistent practice behind. By time they are recognized by the world, hours and days of effort is there in their life. In every aspect of anyone in life nothing but persistent efforts or practice is needed to master something. Someone excelling in studies or a particular skill, incremental improvement is possible before they master only by persistent efforts. We see many start an activity as simple as walking or exercise to reduce weight or achieve health but stop once the motivation is gone. To retain the interest in achieving something, the best way is to write down as to why that particular activity was started and visualizing the ultimate goal of the activity. Daily or periodic revision helps in motivating. More than motivation DISCIPLINE is needed to have consistency in doing something. Nothing was achieved by magic by anyone in life, everyone from their toddler days to old age, have to struggle to learn something new. Basics like walking, talking, riding, reading, are also persistently practiced before mastering the skills. They are done automatically as there are plenty of examples around. But to do something different than others like, singing, playing an instrument, sports, etc., may fail because they'll lose the motivation to do as the talented or benchmarking is not easily available. Lot of single minded dedication is needed to become one and only one to master any skill. Everyone wishes to do well in their areas of interest but many lack the discipline to stick to the activity.

LCD: We have to realize that P^4: PERSISTENT PRACTICE PROMISES PROGRESS. Nothing ever was achieved without following the above formula. We have to commit to do consistently. The best way is to write down as to why we are doing that particular activity and with visualization of end in mind for inspiration, we have to persistently practice with the discipline to progress and achieve the goal for SUCCESSFUL LIVING.

THOUGHT -29

S^3: (PHYSICAL FITNESS)

S^3: STRENGTH, STAMINA, SUPPLENESS

Everyone as long as alive, will have physical body. The day our life goes out of the body, we are dead. BODY IS CALLED TEMPLE because it keeps the soul in it. The physical body is very important as long as we live. Right from birth to death, physical body is the main companion for the soul. The moment soul or the life goes out of the body, it becomes useless and starts decomposing. Hence to keep it fit at any age is very important for all. For every activity we need the help of physical body. Those who cultivate the habit of maintaining the body with exercise and correct nourishment will be living very effectively and efficiently. IF YOU REST YOU RUST. To maintain the physical fitness as we grow older becomes more important. By the age of 30 years the cells which die become more than cells which take birth. Only correct form of exercise or movement will keep the body fit. There are three categories of fitness STRENGTH, STAMINA and SUPPLENESS.

STRENGTH: Strength is for the muscles. The Joints, legs, feet and all are strong because of the muscles cover the bones. The muscular strength is very important to have a fit and sturdy life in later years.

As we age, SARCOPENIA is a problem which effects the muscles and become brittle if not maintained by strengthening. With strength training, the muscles will be become strong and protect other elements like bones and ligaments. More lean body mass or the percentage of muscles in the body facilitates in good metabolism. Good muscles mass in the body makes metabolism work even in sleep. The food gets digested well. Strength training by resistant bands or lifting weights or exercises using self weight of the body like push-ups is very important. Strength training can be compared to a rental income where even in your sleep, the lean body mass percentage of muscle facilitates the digestion of food. Cardio is like a daily wage where you will get paid only when you work.

<u>STAMINA:</u> Stamina is increased by cardio exercises like walking, running, skipping treadmill, elliptical cross trainer. Stamina training is also a fat burning activity but works only while doing it is like a daily wage but more lean body mass muscle is like a rental income where even when sleeping food is digested and calories are burned.

<u>SUPPLENESS</u>: Yoga asanas or basic body bending exercises are important to keep the flexibility of the body to face any eventualities. Yoga asanas are our ancient science of keeping healthy and fit body. Suryanamaskaras are very important for ladies and are excellent to keep them healthy.

LCD: Physical fitness is not one of the above **S**^{3}: STRENGTH, STAMINA, SUPPLENESS, all three are essential to be physically fit. All three have to be included in daily routine to get the maximum benefit of exercise. We need to commit to do all three types of exercises to have a young, healthy and resourceful and fit physical body for SUCCESSFUL LIVING.

THOUGHT -30

SMART: (CHARACTERISTICS OF GOALS)

SMART: SPECIFIC, MEASURABLE, ACHIEVABLE, REALISTIC, TIME BOUND

Everyone has some goals written or unwritten in life at every stage of their lives. Students will have goals to excel in studies and sports, young adults to excel in their career, older to settle well financially and be physically fit and healthy. The goals should not be vague. We need to have a clarity on what to achieve. Here we are going to discuss about the characteristics of goals for anyone at any age.

The clear-cut characteristics will make a goal achievable. For students, if he wants to excel in studies, the percentage he is aiming should be clear. He cannot say that he wants to do well. He should be clear of what he wants 90% or 100%or exactly what percentage. This will make us work backwards and define a route map clearly. For a businessman or employee, what he wants as an earning per month must be defined clearly. This motivates him to achieve the targets. For someone who wants to reduce his weight, how many Kilograms in how many days or months must be specific? For example: In one year (SPECIFIC),wants to reduce 6 kgs

(MEASURABLE), 0.5 kg (ACHIEVABLE), 12 months (REALISTIC) and in one year (TIME BOUND).The goals should be SMART: SPECIFIC, MEASURABLE, ACHIEVABLE, REALISTIC and TIME BOUND. Generally height of a person is stabilized by the age of 20 years. What he can aim is only to alter his weight but never his height. In the same way realistic and achievable should be our goals. We should be able to understand the possible and not possible. There will always be limitations for anyone, we need to understand the limitations and design our life. Someone with few resources cannot do well in short time. The time frame should be practical. Miracles are rare, only practical actions will be fruitful. If someone wants to make money, what we have to give in exchange of services or goods is to be assessed.

LCD: Goals are important for all to have at all stages of life. The goals should have all the characteristics of SMART: SPECIFIC, MEASURABLE, ACHIEVABLE, REALISTIC and TIME BOUND. The word itself says they should be smart to realize. Before planning if you can check whether the goals have all the above characteristics, then automatically SUCCESSFUL LIVING is achieved

THOUGHT -31

SWIFT: (MOST TEMPORARY)

SWIFT: SENSATIONS, WANTS, INTUITIONS, FEELINGS, THOUGHTS

SWIFT: Swift means quickly, as the title says they just go away in a jiffy. Unless we write or repeat they just vanish quickly.

SENSATIONS: Sensation is felt only when we touch something. Travelling in a car, sitting on a Sofa or touching someone or something is felt only till our body or any part of the body is in contact. The moment we are away from it the sensations good or bad will vanish.

WANTS: Every human is a slave of wants. Everyone wants something or the other. Wants are very volatile. They keep on changing. Everyone struggles to fulfill their wants. Be it physical, emotional, social or any area. Even reading this book is for want of knowledge. Right from the day one is born his wants start. The toddler weeps for milk when he is hungry. From then on, the list of wants continues. Only death will stop wants of anyone.

INTUITIONS: In tuition literally means a voice from inside guides us sometimes. Everyone will have the experience of intuition in life. Many times a voice from inside guides us in decision making. Even miscellaneous issues like which route to take to the destination is also guided. Intuition should not be ignored because it helps us to take correct decisions throughout our life.

FEELINGS: Feelings are totally dependent on the external circumstances. Good or bad, like or dislike, love or hate are all some of the feelings or emotions, mostly are the reactions to behavior of others. Though we are subjected to different feelings, they are very volatile. For feelings or emotions to stabilize, we need to reinforce them by repetition.

THOUGHTS: Daily few thousands of thoughts will come to the mind. Mind is continuously inundated with thoughts of all kinds. Many times good ideas in the form of thoughts if not noted down are lost permanently.

LCD: We need to learn that **SWIFT:** SENSATIONS, WANTS, INTUITIONS, FEELINGS, THOUGHTS go off swiftly from the mind. To retain them we need to repeat and reinforce and convert them into actions. This book is trying to give good thoughts but unless converted into actions and repeated actions will be converted to habits. Persistent actions only will produce desired results. We have to let go of the unnecessary thoughts and retain useful ones by noting down, repeating and reproducing. Many times excellent ideas are lost because of not noting or repeating them in mind to remember. In case of wants unless in emergency it is always better to postpone by a day and then if still feel the need, we have to purchase.

THOUGHT -32

SONG: (AREAS FOR HARMONY)

SONG: SOCIETY, ONESELF, NATURE, GOD

There are only four variations or conflicting areas for every human. There may be many other conflicting issues but they will fall in either of the above variations. Our peace of mind, happiness & other positives are directly linked with harmony with these four variations.

SOCIETY: With so many BELIEFS, OPINIONS and CONVICTIONS, AUTHORITY, TRADITION, CULTURES, LANGUAGES etc., there will always be differences with each other. As we all know that world with so many variations, options maintaining harmony seems impossible. Still people have found ways to maintain the harmony with society. One of the best thought is 'AGREE TO DISAGREE'. We have to accept that the interests on many things vary from person to person due to his attitude, experience, environment, education etc,. Agree to Disagree makes one to accept the situations and gives a positive emotion. We should cultivate a habit of genuinely accepting the differences with the society. Perceptions come from attitudes and attitude comes from the thoughts, actions and habits one has acquired.

ONESELF: Surprisingly having conflicts with society, nature and God is understood but they are external factors or areas but conflict with oneself is there always. Right from miscellaneous issues faced in day to day life, decision making is always a challenge with availability of so many options. Waking up to a preset alarm time in the morning is itself is a big task. The moment one is not able to follow his prescheduled routine, it leads to disharmony with one self.

NATURE: Every season carries its merits and demerits. We have a tendency to see only the demerits of the nature and live with displeasure. But if we can accept the variations in nature, the dispute or disharmony will be reduced. We cannot totally accept the nature with its vast variations but the only solution is to accept and live with harmony.

GOD: God as we can sum up as one who is GENERATOR, OPERATOR, DESTROYER. God's creation has so many discrepancies. Why each is unique and different no one has the answer. We find some suffering and some joyful. Some are very poor and others are rich, some are always suffering physically and others with robust health. The list is unending. The best justification seems to be blaming on KARMA, meaning the result of past actions done in our earlier birth. No one can give the reason for such a vast differences existing in the world.

LCD: We need to understand that harmony with the **SONG:** SOCIETY, ONESELF, NATURE, GOD is very important for SUCCESSFUL LIVING

THOUGHT -33

SPCA: (STEPS IN BUSSINESS)

SPCA: SUSPECT, PROSPECT, CLIENT, ADVOCATE

Any relationship, either business or otherwise starts with a pinch of suspicion. Normally unknown relationships take time to build trust. For students in new schools and colleges, for employees in new jobs and for professionals in their initial years of practice have to go through the stages of Suspect, Prospect, Client and Advocate. In personal friendships or relationships like school, colleges or elsewhere, there may not be client and advocate stages but in business or professions the four stages are must to become successful.

To attract the first few prospects in professional practice or business is very difficult. Element of doubt is predominant. Once they cross the barrier of suspicion and become prospects, the responsibility of converting them to clients becomes important. Even after becoming prospects for buying or taking the service, their becoming of clients is not assured. For many the failure happens mostly at the first two stages. Even after attracting a few of them in the initial stages of buying a product or service, making them repeat is herculean task.

Once someone crosses the two stages of suspect and prospect and becomes the client and after few positive experiences and on satisfying with the product or service, will go to the next stage of advocating. We find in business or profession, word of mouth recommendation is most effective method of marketing. Friends, relatives or acquaintances recommendation and opinion is vital in taking decisions. Even to watch a movie, the opinion of others matters hence so many reviewers on movies, hotels etc., Today people bank on the reviews more than anything before taking the service or buying anything.

Even after establishing the business or service the satisfaction of the buyer or the client has become very vital in the successful continuity of the business or profession. With the invasion of the media, the accessibility to reach people is both a boon and curse.

LCD: We should understand that **SPCA:** SUSPECT, PROSPECT, CLIENT, ADVOCATE stages are must to establish in business or profession. We should be very careful at all stages. If the first three stages are taken care, the fourth stage of Advocating is mostly done by others on satisfaction of the product or service. Due to the revolution of the accessibility in reaching people, every care has to be taken to satisfy each and every client or buyer so that he will advocate to others.

We need to understand that the **SPCA:** SUSPECT, PROSPECT, CLIENT, ADVOCATE stages are a must in establishing in business, profession or relationships and have put efforts to lead a SUCCESSFUL LIFE

THOUGHT -34

SAGE: (BLESSINGS)

SAGE: SHASTRA KRUPA, ATMA KRUPA, GURU KRUPA, ESHWARA KRUPA

Krupa or blessings come under the above four categories. We gain knowledge by various means. Books, teachers, gurus and by self realization.

SHASTRA KRUPA: From the day one starts attending to school, the exposure to books and other mediums will start. Earlier it was only by print that the knowledge was available. Today it has many forms like E books, Audio books etc., we need to have respect and confidence in the information present in the book or otherwise, the chances of understanding the information are remote. We need to have full faith on the knowledge that is being given in the form of book or otherwise.

ATMA KRUPA: Confidence on ourselves is needed to learn anything we wish to. We have to have an attitude of learning or knowing the unknown. Our Atma or Soul should have full faith on the knowledge we are trying to learn. Our own blessings are needed for something to understand. If we do not have the confidence on ourselves then the blessings of ourselves is ruled out. We should have full faith, love and confidence on ourselves to learn and understand.

GURU KRUPA: We see many criticizing their teachers or lecturers. No one is ready to take others advise. ADVICE IS SOMETHING WHERE FOOLS DO NOT TAKE IT AND WISE DO NOT NEED IT. So giving advice is useless. That is the reason, to understand something taught by teachers or lecturers or as a matter of fact by anyone who wishes to teach us, we need to have full faith, respect and confidence on them so that the knowledge is easily understood. The blessings of the taught are essential to learn.

ESHWARA KRUPA: Eshwara or God's blessings are the most important for anyone to succeed in life. We have control on our actions to achieve anything but the result is purely on God. Everything in life is happening is only because of God or the creator. The hand which made us has absolute knowledge on our past, present and future life. We should always be grateful to the Eshwara or God who gave us this life. Our parents are the first Gurus or God in the form of humans to guide us in our life. We should always be grateful to the parents for all that we are enjoying in our lives. Unless we have a genuine respect and gratitude on the parents or God, the success in life can be a mirage.

LCD: We need to understand that **SAGE:**SHASTRA KRUPA, ATMA KRUPA, GURU KRUPA, ESHWARA KRUPA the blessings of all the above are essential to gain knowledge. KNOWLEDGE IS MANS GREATEST BEAUTY,

KNOWLEDGE IS HIDDEN TREASURE,

CHIEF OF EARTHY BLESSINGS, BRINGS

CALM, CONTENTMENT, FAME AND PLEASURE.

Gaining and applying the good knowledge facilitates SUUCESSFUL LIVING

THOUGHT -35

THINK: (BEST FILTERS FOR CONVERSATIONS)

THINK: TRUE, HELPFUL, INSPIRING, NECESSARY, KIND

Whenever we speak, elders say we have to THINK before we speak to avoid conflicts. Many times the conflicts are due to what we speak. In the word THINK itself we have filters. The best way to avoid conflicts in speaking is using these filters.

TRUE: We need to check the truthfulness of what we are speaking. Most of the times the hearsay is circulated. The first filter is to check the information for its truthfulness. Unless verified, it is better not to pass on the information to others. Today with revolution in communication through mobile, information is passing on with lightening speed. Lot of fake news is being circulated without being verified.

HELPFUL: Need to check whether the information is helpful for the person receiving it. Useless information only adds up to the garbage in mind. Many times we are exposed to the information which does not help us in any way. With so much communication network, we find it difficult to find the right source of information in case of need. But during a casual conversation care has to be taken about the useful or helpful information.

INSPIRING: Conversation to be fruitful, we need to see whether it is inspiring others in some way. A story or real life incident of successful people always inspires others to perform well in their life. One of the best sources of learning is hearing. Words have a lot of impact. An example: If the word PROBLEM is replaced with the word CHALLENGE, the whole perspective changes. Knowledge and practice are needed to replace the words which inspire.

NECESSARY: Most of the conversations or communications are unnecessary. Almost 80% of the communication will be reduced if we use this filter in our day to day conversations. As written in the THOUGHT 1 ASK: If the words or actions do not improve ATTITUDE, SKILL or KNOWLEDGE, they are unnecessary.

KIND: What we covey has to be kind. Kind words will have a greater impact on others. They totally change the paradigm of the listener. Anything conveyed kindly will have a turbo effect. The words or conversations conveyed LKG: LOVINGLY, KINDLY, GENTLY result in having a greater impact.

LCD: We need to learn that **THINK:** TRUE, HELPFUL, INSPIRING, NECESSARY, KIND filters help us to have effective conversations and by committing to practice will lead to SUCCESSFUL LIVING

THOUGHT -36

TEET: (TIME MANAGEMENT)

TEET: TIME FOR EVERTHINGAND EVERYTHING IN ITS TIME

Among all the resources available like men, material, money, talent, space, and information, time is the only constant. 24 hours per day or 86,400 seconds is what is available to utilize for one to become successful in life. If we are given ₹86,400 daily to spend effectively but unused or unspent has to be returned by the end of the day. I don't think no one will ever waste that money. It is said TIME IS MONEY but since the day comes easily as long as we are alive, people do not realize the value of it to use it to reach whatever they want to achieve in life. All successful people in any field have become what they are by utilization of the resource time very effectively. The first THOUGHT of the book says about ASK: ATTITUDE, SKILL and KNOWLEDGE. If a person uses most of his awaken time to improve their ASK, a day will come where he will be ahead of many to achieve his goals and a successful life. How we use the 86,400 seconds available on daily basis makes all the difference between achiever and non-achiever. Not only hard work but smart work is essential to succeed. At every stage of life, the priorities change. For a student is more for studies. Student needs to prioritize his studies over everything. Every student will have the same amount of time at his disposal but how he uses effectively makes all the difference between a performer and non-performer. For employees, it is how effectively he's doing his assigned job and also keeping himself up-to-date in knowledge with becoming on par with the latest technologies by attending to new courses. In such a fast paced life, the main difference which creates a change in each other is how we utilize the time. Since the time is fixed for all, there should be a TIME TABLE and TIME BOUND GOAL BOOK. TO DO LIST on a daily basis with a TIME TABLE helps a lot in keeping us on track to reach our goals. Short-term goals and long-term goals with a timeframe will help us achieve success. TEET: TIME FOR EVERTHING AND EVERYTHING IN ITS TIME should be planned from a unit of a day to years.

LCD: We should be so conscious of time that it is the only resource which is common to all. No one can have more or less time in their life. Only death can stop us from doing any activity. Once we understand the time is the most important resource, which can create the difference between achiever and non-achiever. We should commit to prioritize our activities on a daily basis which facilitates leading to SUCCESSFUL LIVING.

THOUGHT -37

TWD: (DEFINITION OF PURITY)

TWD: THOUGHT, WORD, DEED

Everyone will have only three types of expressions. Thought, Word and Deed. Thought is subtle, word and deed are gross. Thought itself manifests into word or deed. Thought is the intention behind the word or deed. Thought only motivates to do an action which becomes a habit. Habits define character and character creates our destiny. Thoughts are seeds for any achievement. They are the basis for the attitude of anyone. What we eat is important for physical bodies health and what we think or the thoughts we feed our mind is important for our mental health. Body and Mind are the two most important faculties for anyone. We can easily avoid foods that harm our body because it is very gross and we can understand by our experience or by the advice and experience of others. But when it comes to the mind health, avoiding thoughts which can spoil our peace of mind is very difficult. They can create havoc in the mind. Lot of practice is needed to not to allow thoughts which spoil our happiness and peace of mind. Right from childhood and different stages of life, we are exposed to various people who have their own attitudes. Some may have a habit of criticizing every one, discouraging others or may use abusive language. Every exposure affects the mind if we do not learn to control the mind. All great failures or achievements are the result of thoughts, thoughts to words and deeds. Thought of why only birds can fly and why not humans, have made WRIGHT BOTHERS invent AEROPLANE. All the inventions are the result of someone who thought it is possible and the gross conversions to actions has resulted in the benefit of mankind. When it comes to the human behaviour, the intention is the function of communication. The purity of the person is also defined by the alignment of his THOUGHT, WORD and DEED. But many think differently and express in words contrast to what they think. All the above are examples for the power of thoughts but when it comes to purity of the mind, what we think and say do should be same. Many times we see discord between thoughts, word, and deed. Since thoughts are subtle and cannot be seen, many say or do exactly opposite of what they are thinking, particularly their opinion or themselves, others issues people do not have the same synchrony or alignment of thought, word and deed. For purity of mind which is essential for our peace of mind, we should always see that our thoughts, words and deeds are aligned for SUCCESSFUL LIVING

THOUGHT -38

T^5: (MUST WITH CHILDREN)

T^5: TIME, TALK, TRUST, TOUCH, TRAIN.

All parents and teachers play an important role in society as they have to guide children to become successful in their life and also responsible citizens. We have seen in society that most of the unsuccessful or criminals are the result of bad parenting. The T^5: TIME, TALK, TRUST, TOUCH, TRAIN are to be practiced with children.

TIME: Time has to be given to the children by parents. Since childhood, we have to spare time every day to allow children to express themselves. This allows them to be honest and also share their happiness and sorrows. If they do not have an outlet, the various thoughts will play havoc in their minds. Whatever be the parent situations, sometime of the day, they have to spend time for their kids. That attention should be 100%. It reinforces their minds that parents are there for them at all times.

TALK: Talking is nothing but allowing them or rather cultivating them the habit of sharing all their success and failures. Parents should be good listeners before talking. They need to understand that intention of the child's talk and should be able to appropriately guide them with one to one talk.

Expressing with appropriate words is very important to gain the trust. Parents and Teachers should be an example of what they preach.

TRUST: Trust comes only by empathizing with children. We need to have patience in listening to their experiences and thoughts on daily basis. Trusting them happens only when they can be honest. Unless they have trust on parents, they never will divulge their inner feelings which are essential to guide them to face the challenges of life.

TOUCH: Touch plays a vital role. It gives a tremendous self-confidence. Hugging children till certain age is very important to express our trust and love without words. Sometimes one shake hand or a hug or a kiss on cheek or forehead conveys more than words. The appropriateness is very important here. Particularly during success and failures these gestures work wonders. Once they trust us, training becomes easy.

TRAIN: Systematic training to develop their personality to face the life challenges rests in parents. Parents and teachers play a vital role in shaping up the character of the children.

LCD: All parents and teachers need to remember T^5: TIME, TALK, TRUST, TOUCH, TRAIN to be followed with children. It is easy to remember these five and be conscious of them while dealing with children. This will help the society in whole and it will lead the students to live SUCCESSFULLY.

THOUGHT -39

T^2M^3SI: (RESOURCES)

T^2M^3SI: TIME, TALENT, MONEY, MEN, MATERIAL, SPACE, INFORMATION

Effective and efficient usage of resources leads to success in life. There are fixed and variable resources. We hear people complaining about lack of resources to become successful. We say some are born with Golden spoon or Silver spoon. It only indicates the material wealth they possess. But success is not measured only in possession of material wealth alone. Talented people achieve success and material wealth is a byproduct. We see inspiring stories where people born in poverty reaching pinnacle of success in their chosen field. For everyone to reach their goals the resources available are T^2M^3SI: TIME, TALENT, MONEY, MEN, MATERIAL, SPACE, INFORMATION

TIME: Though Time is constant for all, all other resources are variable. Time being a constant resource and a very important one in every one's life, how we use our time creates a wide difference in the success of each other. A student, to start with is a best example. We see that one who utilizes the time for studies will excel in that phase of life. Though the utilization of that resource makes a difference at all phases of life, at the student phase it reflects more.

TALENT: Talent is unique for each individual. We have seen Sports persons, Actors, Musicians, Musical Instruments players etc., using their uniqueness in achieving success in life. One who can realize his talent at an early age will become more successful. One unique talent exhibited at the right place and right time will make one successful.

MONEY: Money is other major resource for success particularly in business. Money makes money. With availability of other resources but lack of money may not take one forward in life. Nowadays potential new business ideas are being encouraged by the Venture Capitalists in funding the young talent.

MEN: Apart from availability of other resources, skilled men / women is essential to run and become successful in manufacturing or service sectors. Mere Ideas are not sufficient, skilled persons to execute the ideas are very important resource.

MATERIAL: Availability of material is another resource. Many industries are successful because of the exploitation of locally available raw material to convert to finished goods. For any industry to be successful availability of raw material & transport of finished goods with minimum cost is essential. Transport facility also comes under material resource.

SPACE: For anything to become successful, space is essential. Space is needed to plan the placement of other resources. Effective utilization of space & effective utilization of men/women is vital for success of the business venture.

INFORMATION: Without information, having all the other resources will be in vain. For everything information is vital. Knowledge of the business or the service is the most important resource.

LCD: There are only **T^{2}M^{3}SI**: TIME, TALENT, MONEY, MEN, MATERIAL, SPACE, INFORMATION resources in the world to use and be successful in life. We have to gain sufficient knowledge to procure and use the above resources and commit to execute the plan for SUCESSFUL LIVING

THOUGHT -40

WATCH: (ULTIMATE PHILOSOPHY)

WATCH: WORKHARD, AIM HIGH, TRUST IN GOD, CULTIVATE CHRACTER, HOPE FOR THE BEST

This is the best chapter to conclude for success in life.

WORKHARD: We keep hearing since our childhood during all stages of life to work hard. Today not only work hard but also smart work is needed. A focused hard work with end in view is the best way. It is called working backwards. Imagining with image of success is one of the best methods in achieving the goals. Hard work with smart and effective approach is needed.

AIM HIGH: We should always Aim high. There is story: A person will be catching Fish. One man keeps observing this person. Whenever he catches a big fish, he is throwing into the water and small fish are kept in the basket. This surprises the person and he approaches and asks the reason. The fish catcher replies that his vessel used for cooking is small hence he is throwing the big fish. We should realize that our potential to achieve is unlimited. We should always aim high in all stages of our life and in all areas of our life. An attitude of MOST & MORE is very good to achieve. We should be happy with existing stage but wish to achieve Most & More. A state of Mind of MORE THAN ENOUGH.

<u>TRUST IN GOD</u>: As we observe that efforts are in our hands, we can try our best to work hard to progress in any field but the existential power is felt. The result is always in the hands of the invisible power, we call GOD. Trust in the power is very essential. We should do our work with devotion and trust the God or the creator.

<u>CULTIVATE CHARACTER</u>: In spite of material success, the character is very important for a peaceful and resourceful life. We should always see that TWD: Thought, Word & Deed are aligned. If money is lost nothing is lost, if health is lost something is lost but if character is lost everything is lost in life. A person is genuinely respected by his character alone. In spite of achieving material success a person without character is never respected by society.

<u>HOPE FOR THE BEST:</u> Always Hope for the best. We should never leave two ropes in despair HOPE & FAITH. Hope and faith give us tremendous strength in times of failure

LCD:

Remember WATCH: Work hard, Aim High, Trust in God, Cultivate Character, Hope for the best at all times. Make it your life mantra. This philosophy is ultimate to do well in life and is best sum up of many principles of success available.

It is easy to remember this KISS format of THOUGHT as it is always with us on the wrist.

All the very best for SUCCESSFUL LIVING